The Making of the Middle East

The Iranian Revolution and the Resurgence of Islam

The Making
of the
Middle East

The Iranian Revolution and the Resurgence of Islam

Barry Rubin

Mason Crest Publishers
Philadelphia

Frontispiece: Flag-waving Iranians at a demonstration marking the 28th anniversary of the Islamic revolution, February 11, 2007, Tehran.

Produced by OTTN Publishing, Stockton, N.J.

Mason Crest Publishers
370 Reed Road
Broomall, PA 19008
www.masoncrest.com

First printing

1 3 5 7 9 8 6 4 2

Library of Congress Cataloging-in-Publication Data

Rubin, Barry M.
  The Iranian revolution and the resurgence of Islam / Barry Rubin.
      p. cm. — (The making of the Middle East)
  Includes bibliographical references and index.
  ISBN-13: 978-1-4222-0174-9
  ISBN-10: 1-4222-0174-0
  1. Iran—Politics and government—1979–1997. 2. Iran—Politics and government—1997– 3.
Islam and politics—Iran. I. Title.
  DS318.9.R83 2008
  955.05'42—dc22
                                    2007029077

Table of Contents

Introduction:
The Importance of the Middle East

The region known as the Middle East has a significant impact on world affairs. The countries of the greater Middle East—the Arab states of the Arabian Peninsula, Eastern Mediterranean, and North Africa, along with Israel, Turkey, Iran, and Afghanistan—possess a large portion of the world's oil, a valuable commodity that is the key to modern economies. The region also gave birth to three of the world's major faiths: Judaism, Christianity, and Islam.

In recent years it has become obvious that events in the Middle East affect the security and prosperity of the rest of the world. But although such issues as the wars in Iraq and Afghanistan, the floundering Israeli-Palestinian peace process, and the struggles within countries like Lebanon and Sudan are often in the news, few Americans understand the turbulent history of this region.

Human civilization in the Middle East dates back more than 8,000 years, but in many cases the modern conflicts and issues in the region can be attributed to events and decisions made during the past 150 years. In particular, after World War I ended in 1918, the victorious Allies—especially France and Great Britain—redrew the map of the Middle East, creating a number of new countries, such as Iraq, Jordan, and Syria. Other states, such as Egypt and Iran, were dominated by foreign powers until after the Second World War. Many of the Middle Eastern countries did not become independent until the 1960s or 1970s. Political and economic developments in the Middle Eastern states over the past four decades have shaped the region's direction and led to today's headlines.

The purpose of the MAKING OF THE MIDDLE EAST series is to nurture a better understanding of this critical region, by providing the basic history along

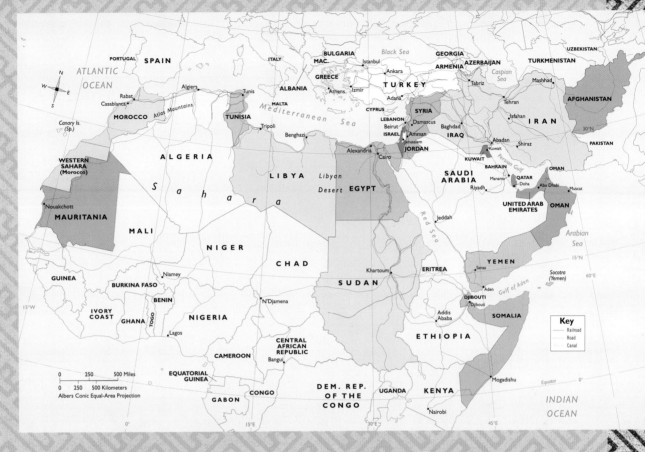

with explanation and analysis of trends, decisions, and events. Books will examine important movements in the Middle East, such as the development of nationalism in the 1880s and the rise of Islamism from the 1970s to the present day.

The 10 volumes in the MAKING OF THE MIDDLE EAST series are written in clear, accessible prose and are illustrated with numerous historical photos and maps. The series should spark students' interest, providing future decision-makers with a solid foundation for understanding an area of critical importance to the United States and the world.

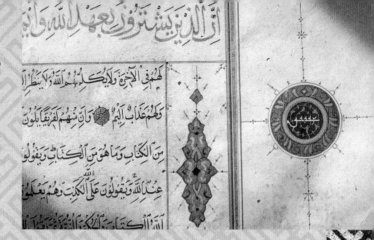

(Opposite) A view of the Great Mosque, Mecca, Saudi Arabia. The birthplace of the prophet Muhammad, Mecca is Islam's holiest city. (Right) A page from the Qur'an, Islam's scriptures. Muslims believe the Qur'an represents the actual words of God, as dictated to Muhammad by the angel Gabriel.

1 *The What and the Why of Islamism*

Islam has existed for almost 1,400 years, but the radical Islamist political philosophy is a modern creation. Islamists cite specific passages in the Qur'an, Islam's holy book; sayings of Muhammad, the religion's founding prophet; actions taken during the early years of Islam; and Islamic theologians of the Middle Ages. But theirs is a highly selective reading that is often at variance with Islam as it was practiced over the centuries. Islamism is a political creed, a response to very modern problems.

The Expansion of Islam

Shortly after it began in the early seventh century, the religion of Islam enjoyed remarkable military and political successes. Consolidating its base of support in the cities of Medina and then Mecca, on the Arabian Peninsula in what is today the Kingdom of Saudi Arabia, Islam spread further by its direct appeal. Its rituals are simple and accessible to people of all backgrounds, and Islam does not have a hierarchical authority structure. Even more significant in the spread of Islam, however, was the fact that Arab Muslim armies defeated both the Byzantine and Persian empires, the latter in 637. Almost overnight, in historical terms, an extensive empire was created. It stretched from Afghanistan in the east, through the Fertile Crescent, Egypt and North Africa, all the way to Spain in the west.

To Muslims, this expansion seemed like a miracle, though it was aided by the fact that the political rivals defeated by the Arabs were already weak and demoralized. Nevertheless, success on the battlefield made Islam a mighty power in both religious and political terms, a factor that has lasted down to the present day. By various means of pressure and benefits—many of them economic—the great majority of the local non-Arab people were so thoroughly converted to the new religion that they would thereafter generally act as if they had never had any other previous identity.

How would the Muslim people be governed? As long as Muhammad had been alive, he was the clear leader, combining in himself both religious

The Umayyad Mosque, shown here at night, was built in Damascus, Syria, between 706 and 715 by the rulers of Islam's first dynasty. After the death of Muhammad in 632, controversy erupted over who should succeed him as Islam's leader. Within three decades, the Umayyad family had taken power, but many Muslims were unhappy with that outcome. This ultimately led to the rupture of Islam into the majority Sunni and the minority Shia branches.

and political functions. After his death he was followed by four caliphs who also held—at least nominally—these two functions.

Golden Age?

In retrospect, many Muslims view this era as a "golden age," the peak of their religion's piety as well as worldly success. Most significantly for today, it is this time that Islamists idealize and to which they wish to return. Indeed, political Islamism claims legitimacy by arguing that this era of perceived high piety, close adherence to Islam's religious tenets, and Islam's political domination forms the proper model for living in and governing current society. In comparison, the last 1,200 years of the actual functioning of the societies and polities in which Muslims live has been a deviation.

Was the golden age indeed so wonderful? Three of the first four caliphs were assassinated, and the Muslim lands were repeatedly ripped by civil war, sometimes among factions with differing theological views. The most important and lasting split—between the Sunni and Shia—was due to an early disagreement about who should be the caliph. By the early 660s, just three decades after the death of Muhammad, the Umayyad dynasty ruled from Damascus. Especially ironic was the fact that this family had been among the leading opponents of Islam and its founding prophet in the first place.

It should be added, though, that these facts are much better known among Western scholars than among Muslim believers. Historical inquiry and the critical examination of sources—especially about Islam's early period—have been generally discouraged in Muslim lands. The myth of a political golden age when all were pious and everything went well for Muslims is deeply entrenched, furnishing ammunition for contemporary political Islamists who view this period as the basis for a modern-day utopia.

After the eighth century a series of dynasties followed, and over the centuries the original unified caliphate was divided into sometimes warring states. The caliph (religious leader) and the sultan (political ruler) were usually two titles held by a single person, but in practice the role of sultan was primary.

Thus, the history of religion and politics in Muslim lands during the Middle Ages was roughly parallel to that in the West. Religious authorities had great power, but it was the state and its kings or sultans that prevailed in the actual governing of the people. The same applies to law, with religious law nominally in command but with the law set by state, nobles, and customs playing the more important role. Indeed, the intellectual and cultural peak of the Muslim states, during the Abbasid caliphate in Baghdad 1,000 years ago, was characterized by a libertine court in which poetry celebrated the joys of eroticism and wine.

The Triumph of Islamic Conservatism

After the Middle Ages, the trajectory of intellectual and technological development in the West and in the Muslim world differed dramatically. In the Christian-dominated West, beginning around the year 1400, there was an age of invention, development, exploration, and colonization coupled with the Reformation, Renaissance, and Enlightenment. The political and worldly power of religious institutions declined, while secular thought pushed back the power of religion to restrict free inquiry.

By way of contrast, in the Muslim lands conservative theologians prevailed. In the 11th century Ibn Salah al-din al-Shahrouzi issued a fatwa, or legal decree handed down by an Islamic religious leader, banning the study of logic as a "heresy delivering man into Satan's bosom." The advocates of such ideas favored the narrowest possible reading of Muslim texts, in opposition to thinkers who tried to analyze these texts using the tools of comparison and logic. The former, victorious school preached, in the words of the contemporary Egyptian liberal thinker Tarek Heggy, "a dogmatic adherence to the letter rather than the spirit of religion [which slammed] the doors shut in the face of rationality."

The rulers of the day preferred the conservative approach, which stamped down on dissent and defended the status quo against liberals who

Young boys in Baghdad, Iraq, study the Qur'an. From the Middle Ages on, Muslims have been discouraged from interpreting the rules found in the Qur'an, and in other early Islamic sources, to fit modern conditions.

raised subversive questions. Consequently, the gates of *ijtihad*—letting qualified scholars debate the reinterpretation of religious texts to fit new times and situations—were closed. Creative thinking or critical inquiry regarding the meaning of the Qur'an and later religious texts was forbidden. Only rulings already made and narrowly adhered to would be acceptable.

The greatest irony is that it had been Europeans who heeded the rationalist Islamic scholars of the Middle Ages in their revival of classical Greek thought. Thus, these Muslim scholars helped pave the way for Europe's great cultural and scientific progress while being forgotten by their own people. In the West, rationalists defeated dogmatists. The backward Middle Ages had given way to the Renaissance and Reformation. Had the same side won in Europe as in the Middle East, Heggy noted, Europe today would be at a far lower stage of development and enlightenment.

Yet even this does not tell the whole story. In practice, Muslim politics and society were highly conservative but also evinced a strong pragmatic streak. Traditional Islam as it was practiced for a thousand years preferred that Muslims live under a Muslim ruler. Such a ruler, however, would be acceptable as long as he could be considered reasonably pious and he did not interfere with religious practice.

It was further accepted that Muslim clerics should stay clear of politics. Religious observance was strong but not generally compelled in any detail or with a great degree of strictness. It was forbidden to accuse other Muslims, except in the most extreme and rare circumstances, of being heretical. Existing customs, including pre-Islamic ones or local traditional interpretations, were accepted.

The fact that traditional Islam as actually practiced was and is distinct from Islamism is a point of the greatest importance, the key factor explaining why most Muslims have not accepted Islamism as their political doctrine. At the same time, many Islamist arguments meet with more approval because they can claim to be consistent with widely accepted principles. This explains why Islamism is as popular as it has been among Muslims. For example, mainstream Muslim clerics would once have laughed at any notion that suicide terrorist attacks were religiously proper. But now, due to the pressure and persuasion of Islamist groups, such attacks are increasingly accepted as conforming to Islam.

Defining Islamism

What, then, is political Islam or Islamism? In content it is an interpretation of Islam—and by far not the only possible one—directed at a political goal. Most important, it is a revolutionary political ideology, parallel to such systematic programs as communism and fascism, liberal democracy and nationalism.

The main concepts of Islamism, though they vary in detail, include the following:

Islam provides all the elements needed by both society and polity.
As a result, it should be the commanding source of ideas and laws. This notion is embodied in a common Islamist slogan, "Islam is the answer." Ultimately, humans have no right to choose their systems or laws because God has done so for them. Their job is merely to adhere to God's will.

"Islam is the answer" reads this banner in Gaza City. Islamists, who reject Western approaches to social and political questions, are especially hostile to the separation of religion and governance. In their view, Islam must form the foundation for public as well as private life.

Only a proper Islam is suitable as the governing doctrine. This means a strict view based on how the founders and early disciples of Islam would have interpreted it.

All the states where Muslims live—with the possible exception of Iran—and their societies are in a condition of *jahiliyya*, meaning they are equivalent to the pre-Muslim pagan societies. Thus, they must be thoroughly purged and transformed. This concept challenges traditional mainstream Islam—implying, for example, that the great majority of clerics are not practicing or teaching Islam properly. In the minds of mainstream Muslims, the idea of professing Muslims being in a state of *jahiliyya* is equally heretical.

all, Muslims had thought themselves properly religious for centuries without ever acting as the Islamists prescribed. The great clerics of the past had preached cooperation with the authorities or passivity until the messiah returned to put the world right.

Others who consider themselves Muslims and practice the main tenets of the religion may in fact be pagans. *Takfir*, the practice of declaring someone an unbeliever, is especially controversial. Since apostasy from Islam is punishable by death, this idea implies—and is meant to—that it is just and proper to kill such people.

Jihad is an active duty. Today the great majority of Muslims accept the idea that jihad means a struggle against non-Muslims to increase the area under the rule of Islam, but they have treated it as an archaic concept, something not suitable for the modern world. In contrast, Islamists seek to use jihad to mobilize revolutionary forces.

The strictest form of mainstream Islam widely practiced, the Wahhabi version that dominates in Saudi Arabia and Qatar, is not in itself Islamist. Saudi Arabia is really a traditional state in Muslim terms, given that the religious and political authorities are quite separate though the religious ones have much influence and the political ones have strong Islamic credentials. Islamists are not happy with Saudi Arabia as their model. Indeed, Osama bin

An anti-Israel demonstration in Dhaka, Bangladesh, September 2006.
Support for the Palestinians and opposition to Israel has been a mainstay
of public opinion throughout the Muslim world.

Laden began as an Islamist revolutionary seeking to overthrow the Saudi regime. But Wahhabism can be a portal to Islamism in other countries by leading individuals toward a stricter, less tolerant, form of Islam.

In short, Islamism is a political ideology that seeks to seize state power and transform existing societies. It says that the answer to the problems of countries where Muslims live is not tradition or nationalism or liberal democratic pragmatism, but only the rule of a strictly interpreted version of Islam. It seeks the overturning of existing regimes, by violence or other means. It views all the problems of Muslim countries and societies as being created by the West and Israel or their local, superficially Muslim collaborators. It rejects Western approaches to political or social issues but not necessarily Western technology. It demands the defeat of Western political or cultural influences and the destruction of Israel. In this context, it argues that victory is easy if Muslims are only united, willing to fight, and ready to sacrifice their lives.

Beyond this basic analysis and program, many issues are left open by Islamism. No one state, movement, or leader furnishes a model. Islamists may view Iran or the former Taliban regime in Afghanistan in a positive or negative light. There are both Sunni and Shia Islamists, and they may champion the cause of their denomination and hate the other one. Islamists may or may not favor a leading role for clerics.

Also left open are questions of revolutionary strategy and tactics. On the tactical level, many Islamist movements have embraced armed struggle and terrorism, but this is by no means the only choice. Depending on the specific group and circumstances, Islamist groups can be involved in grassroots organizing and even elections. As for strategy, some put the priority on overthrowing the local regime, as a stepping-stone toward destroying Israel and defeating the West. Others, like bin Laden, put the emphasis on attacking the West and Israel as a requirement for bringing down their own rulers.

It is by no means inevitable that Islamism will triumph, either among Muslims in general or in any specific country. Since the 1979 Iranian Revolution—and with temporary exceptions in Sudan and Afghanistan—no Islamist regime has successfully seized power. The strength of existing regimes and the hostility or indifference of the majority of Muslims has prevented such an outcome. Nevertheless, Islamism has clearly become the main opposition force throughout the Arab world and in countries as diverse as Nigeria and Indonesia. In the early 21st century, following the collapse of communism, it is also the leading alternative ideology to liberal democratic thought.

(Opposite) Ayatollah Ruhollah Khomeini waves to supporters following his return to Iran from exile, February 1, 1979. "[Muhammad] brought the glad tidings that we [Muslims] are going to conquer the entire world and destroy everybody," Khomeini would announce. (Right) Mohammad Reza Pahlavi, photographed with his wife, Empress Farah, was deposed by the Iranian Revolution.

2 The Rise of Islamism and the Iranian Revolution

Islamism is a reaction to the dislocations of modern times, the impact of Western ideas, and the perceived failure of other political philosophies in places where Muslims live. Its appeal is felt especially in the Middle East, but Islamism also has found supporters in such places as Indonesia, Malaysia, and Chechnya.

Only in recent years has Islamism attracted much attention from the Western media. However, its roots are many decades old.

The Muslim Brotherhood

Most directly, Islamism can be traced to the founding of the Egyptian Muslim Brotherhood by Hasan al-Banna in 1928. The Brotherhood proposed to put Egypt under an Islamic regime based on Muslim law. The movement emphasized mass organizing but also had a secret armed group that assassinated political figures. Banna himself was killed in 1949, presumably by Egyptian government agents. After the Muslim Brotherhood attempted to assassinate Gamal Abdel Nasser, Egypt's president, Nasser's regime harshly suppressed the movement in the 1950s. By then, however, the Brotherhood had spread to other places, notably Jordan, Syria, and among the Palestinians.

The most important ideologue of the Muslim Brotherhood was the Egyptian scholar Sayyid Qutb. He developed the idea that contemporary society in Muslim countries was comparable to the pre-Islamic era of *jahiliyya* and hence was illegitimate. Thus, it was possible for him to redefine jihad not so much as a struggle to spread Islam to non-Muslim lands but as a struggle to revolutionize and purify countries that were already Muslim. Qutb was executed by Nasser's government in 1966.

Yet during the 1950s and 1960s, the role of Islam in politics was mainly as a conservative force seeking to preserve traditional society. Its enemy was the Arab nationalist movements and regimes that seemed to be taking over the Arab world at that time. Since these forces were socialist, secularist, and allied with the Soviet Union, Islamic groups were sponsored by countries like Saudi Arabia and Jordan, which wanted the groups to fight against revolutionary change.

Throughout most of the 1970s, Islamist movements were gradually developing. For example, the Egyptian Muslim Brotherhood ran candidates for parliament indirectly and campaigned for imposing Sharia (Muslim law) as the basis for Egyptian law. In Syria, the local Brotherhood organized against the government.

The Islamic Revolution in Iran

In 1979 events in Iran electrified Islamists throughout the Middle East. Early that year, following months of protests, the regime of the U.S.-backed shah, Mohammad Reza Pahlavi, was ousted. While diverse elements of Iranian society had helped topple the shah, the leadership of a radical Shia cleric, Ayatollah Ruhollah Khomeini, proved crucial. Khomeini and his Islamist allies soon consolidated power, transforming Iran into a conservative Islamic theocracy.

Just as the Russian Revolution of the early 20th century had shaped the Left for decades thereafter, so did the success of the 1979 Iranian Revolution shape Islamist movements throughout the Middle East in its aftermath. Even when Islamist groups had no loyalty to—or even liking for—Tehran, the fact that the Iranians showed that a revolution of this sort could happen provided plentiful inspiration. Moreover, many of the Islamist groups held ideas that paralleled the thinking of Ayatollah Khomeini.

If Qutb was to the Islamist revolution what Karl Marx was to communism, then Khomeini was Islamism's Vladimir Lenin. According to Khomeini, there existed a worldwide struggle between the forces of Islam and those of corrupt materialism. In this struggle, he said, every Muslim must take sides. The Muslim masses must be mobilized to fight the West, and

Western conceptions of freedom and social organization must be rejected. Moreover, he claimed that all existing regimes in Muslim-populated countries were illegitimate and should be overthrown.

The appeal of Iran's Islamic revolution also came at a time when the dominant force in the Arab world, Arab nationalism, was becoming increasingly discredited. The Arab nationalists had failed to drive out Western influence, destroy Israel, unite the Arab world, or provide rapid economic development and higher living standards. The atmosphere is well conveyed in the words of Professor Hisham Sharabi in 1985: "Today the Arab reality and the Arab dream appear separated by an unbridgeable gap. The hope that has animated the past generation's struggle . . . turned into cynicism and despair. . . . Power-holders throughout the Arab world seem to have found it fairly easy to get away with the contradiction between their verbal and actual behavior."

Into this moment of despair burst the Iranian Revolution's promise of a dramatic alternative offering total victory. A sense of this message's power can be gleaned from a 1987 sermon by Khomeini. Islam, he said then, "has answers for the needs of men from the beginning to the end . . . for daily [life], and for issues that might arise in the future and about which we know nothing now. . . . [It] satisfies all the material, spiritual, philosophical, and mystical needs of all humanity at all times until Judgment Day." If Muhammad had stayed home and preached, Khomeini claimed, "we would have followed his example." Instead, the Prophet launched "an armed struggle and established a government. He then sent missionaries and representatives everywhere. . . . He brought the glad tidings that we are going to conquer the entire world and destroy everybody." Muslims today should imitate Muhammad, Khomeini said. "He set up a government, we should do the same. He participated in various wars, we should do the same. He defended Islam, we should also defend it." Muslims have a duty to fight to put this regime into authority everywhere in the world, Khomeini maintained.

Khomeini was no mere impractical fanatic. He had outmaneuvered all rivals and proven himself a man of action, among the century's most successful politicians in mobilizing millions of people with his vision through demagoguery, ideology, and organization. In addition, he was blessed with shrewd, capable lieutenants who immediately started building institutions to ensure that the Islamic revolutionaries stayed in power. They proved relatively cautious—compared to their fiery rhetoric—about directly subverting their neighbors because they realized that this could endanger the revolution's survival at home.

But Khomeini's intention was to convince other Muslims to make a violent revolution. He regarded Iran as only the first step to creating a utopian Islamic empire that would bring, in his words, "absolute perfection and infinite glory and beauty." He urged Muslims: "Rise up! Grab what is yours by right through nails and teeth! Do not fear the propaganda of the superpowers and their sworn stooges. Drive out the criminal rulers! . . . March towards an Islamic government!" If only all Muslims cooperated, they would be "the greatest power on earth."

If relative backwardness was due to the shortcomings of local cultural or political traditions, these must be changed to be more like Western ones in order to achieve modernization. The road to development would be long and hard. If, however, the essential problem was external, this meant that progress could only be attained by defeating Western "imperialism."

One of the shah's main crimes, according to Khomeini, was linking progress to Westernization. In pre-revolutionary Iran, as elsewhere in the Middle East, tradition was unfashionable, while things Western were seen as representing progress. Indifference to religion, Khomeini charged, was taken to be a symbol of civilization, while piety was a sign of backwardness to elites who would rather be tourists in Europe than pilgrims in Mecca.

To make matters worse from Khomeini's standpoint, this Western cultural invasion was also popular in many ways. People wanted cheaper, better-quality goods and liberating ideas. Assertions of defiance barely concealed a nagging conviction that Western ascendancy was inevitable and that one might as well join the winning side.

Showdown with the United States

Khomeini thus had good reason to consider the United States, which was already the greatest power on earth, to be the most dangerous enemy of his ambitions. The United States, of course, had been a mainstay for the shah, whom he had overthrown. Yet Khomeini's problem was that Iranians liked or feared America so much that they did not want to fight against its influence. Even many of his top aides wanted to compromise with Washington, following an Iranian tradition of appeasing the strongest foreign power. They publicly denounced the United States, then secretly asked it for money, support, and favors.

The ayatollah feared that this U.S. leverage might temper his revolution by supporting moderate factions against militant ones—or might overthrow the revolution altogether. And he knew that Washington would do everything in its power to prevent the spread of Islamic revolution to Saudi Arabia and the other monarchies of the Persian Gulf.

Thus, Khomeini and his most radical followers wanted a decisive break with the United States to eliminate its influence and to show Iran's people

Iranian demonstrators hold aloft an effigy of Jimmy Carter, the U.S. president, during a large rally in Tehran, December 1979. By this time, Iran and the United States were embroiled in a bitter dispute over the seizure of the American embassy staff in Tehran.

that it could not defeat the Islamic revolution. Anti-Americanism would then be a useful device to rally the masses around the new regime. But Khomeini, and many other Islamists, also firmly believed that the United States was a satanic force preventing utopia on earth, deliberately keeping most of the world backward.

These are the reasons why Iranian militants stormed the U.S. embassy in Tehran in November 1979, kidnapped its staff, and held most of them hostage until January 1981. Khomeini called this a "second revolution," which would banish forever Iranians' servility toward the United States. "For centuries," Khomeini said, Western propaganda "made all of us believe that it is impossible to resist." Now, he rejected compromise because he wanted to show that the United States could do nothing against Iran, that its strength was an illusion.

The revolution could be made safe only by cutting contacts with the United States—"the center for world imperialism," Iran's ambassador to the U.N. called it—which "can under no circumstances" be trusted. The powerful speaker of parliament Ali Akbar Hashemi Rafsanjani boasted, "Today we don't make any decisions, great or small, under the influence of foreign powers [including] a blasphemous country like the Soviet Union or an imperialist aggressive country like America."

Thus, Iran's rulers saw the American hostage crisis in practical terms. The radicals used it to displace moderates in the regime and unite the country around themselves. At first, the imbroglio cost Iran almost nothing. Iran did not need the United States. It could still sell oil to others. Khomeini correctly calculated that Iran could thumb its nose at both the United States and the Soviet Union, knowing the superpower rivals would prevent each other from attacking him.

But Khomeini was not interested in merely being on the defensive. He thought the hostage crisis was an Iranian victory over the United States that would inspire Muslim revolt against the West. Each day the hostages were held, Washington's credibility would fall among Iran's people and among the Gulf Arabs. Iran was in no hurry to make a deal. Negotiations went slowly, intermediaries made no progress, and the Western media counted off the number of days of "America held hostage."

The Iran-Iraq War

Khomeini was militarily challenged, however, not by the United States but by his Muslim neighbors in Iraq. That country's dictator, Saddam Hussein, attacked Iran in September 1980 because, on the one hand, he saw it as being weak. Having gone through so much disorder and purged its own army, Iran might crumble before an Iraqi invasion. And since Tehran had expelled its American protector and so totally isolated itself, Saddam reasoned, it could expect no outside help.

On the other hand, Saddam was also prompted to attack Iran because its Islamism seemed so strong. Saddam had no intention of letting Iran foment a revolution to make itself master of the Gulf, much less overthrow his own government. Tehran was doing its best to foment an Iraqi Shia uprising, sponsoring an assassination attempt on Iraq's foreign minister and other terrorist acts. Iraq's already restive Shia majority might respond by rebelling against the ruling Sunni minority.

The mother of an Iraqi soldier killed in the early weeks of the war with Iran kisses Saddam Hussein, the Iraqi dictator, 1980. Saddam's expectation of a quick victory over Iran proved a costly miscalculation; the war would drag on for eight years.

Even before Iran's revolution, Iraqi Shias had been organizing revolutionary cells. Shia underground groups ambushed government officials and bombed offices. Demonstrations broke out in the Shia holy cities at the annual processions marking the martyrdom of Hussein, the grandson of the prophet Muhammad. Iranian propaganda compared Saddam to the Sunni Umayyad ruler Yazid, who had killed Hussein at Karbala some 1,300 years earlier. The crowds chanted, "Saddam, remove your hand! The people of Iraq do not want you!" A popular young Shia cleric, Baqr al-Sadr, was a prime candidate to be Iraq's Khomeini.

But Saddam's regime struck back with ferocious repression. About 600 clerics and activists were shot, including al-Sadr and his sister. Iraq also deported more than 200,000 ethnic Persians, who might conceivably be supportive of Iran.

While repressing the Shia opposition, Saddam also wooed Iraq's Shias by promoting more of them to top posts in the government, in his ruling Baath Party, and in the army. They were, he reminded them in speech after speech, Iraqis by citizenship and Arabs by ethnicity. "God destined the Arabs to play a vanguard role in Islam," he ingeniously explained, so "any contradiction between a revolution which calls itself Islamic and the Arab revolution means that the revolution is not Islamic." Tehran's real inspiration was said to be Zionism, "Persianism," and the reactionary concepts of "the Khomeini gang."

On September 22, 1980, Saddam ordered his army to march into Iran, expecting a quick, easy victory that would make him master of the Gulf and the entire Arab world. Instead it was the start of a bloody, protracted war that cost both countries dearly. The fighting would seesaw for eight years, reducing the two prosperous states to near-bankruptcy. The conflict would be a struggle for supremacy and survival between two dictators indifferent to casualties, and two systems—radical Arab nationalism and revolutionary Islamism—that were each determined to destroy the other. Iran encouraged its warriors to seek martyrdom. "The path of jihad is the path to heaven," said Radio Tehran. But in the end neither side would win a clear victory.

Iraqi soldiers celebrate the cease-fire in the Iran-Iraq War, July 1988. The brutal conflict had claimed as many as a million lives.

Finally, in July 1988, Iran and Iraq accepted a cease-fire brokered by the United Nations. It went into effect the following month.

Afghanistan and Beyond

Aside from Iran's revolution, the other event that most contributed to the new Islamism was the war in Afghanistan. Taking advantage of the U.S. setback in Iran, the Soviet Union invaded Afghanistan in 1979 to back up a Communist coup there. Afghans supported by foreign Muslim volunteers, armed by the United States and financed by Saudi Arabia, fought a long guerrilla war against the Soviet army and its local allies. Soviet forces finally pulled out of Afghanistan in early 1989.

One of the key advocates of using Afghanistan as a model for worldwide Islamist revolution was Abdallah Azzam. A Palestinian educator, he worked in Jordan and later played an important part in building the Arab Islamist forces fighting in Afghanistan, where he was killed. Azzam's most faithful disciple was a wealthy Saudi named Osama bin Laden. Helped by the growing domestic crisis in the Soviet Union—which would soon lead to the collapse of the Communist regime in Moscow—the Islamist mujahedin (those who wage holy war) overthrew the Communist regime in Afghanistan.

Now Islamists were intoxicated with their seeming victories. They claimed to have defeated both superpowers and to have overthrown a powerful regime in Iran. There was nothing, they argued, that Islamism could not achieve. Arab veterans of the Afghan war headed home with the goal of making more revolutions. Under the Taliban regime, which took power in 1996, Afghanistan became a safe haven and base for these Islamists.

In the Philippines, a long battle to create a Muslim state in the south heated up in the 1990s, particularly with the 1993 founding of the Abu Sayyaf group, which used terrorism to intimidate opponents. In another part of

This photo shows the funeral of two sisters, ages 13 and 12, who were killed after Chechen separatists seized a school in Beslan, Russia. More than 330 people, many of them children, died in the September 2004 incident. Independence for predominantly Muslim Chechnya became a popular cause among Islamists worldwide.

Asia, Islamist terrorists in the disputed Jammu and Kashmir area under Indian control also used terrorism to make life impossible for non-Muslims in the region. Noteworthy were the Lashkar-e-Toiba terrorist group, founded in 1993, and the Jaish-e-Mohammed, established seven years later.

Meanwhile, in Russia, Chechnyan separatists adapted Islamist ideology and terrorist methods in the late 1990s. They also extended their attacks to other parts of Russia, believing that killing civilians might persuade Moscow to give up and grant them independence. In December 2001, a group of Chechen terrorists, including widows who had lost their husbands in the struggle with Russia, kidnapped the entire audience in a Moscow theater. A botched rescue attempt by Russian commandos resulted in the death of hundreds of hostages. In another wave of attacks beginning in August 2004, Chechen terrorists carried out the simultaneous bombing of two Russian airliners; detonated a bomb at a Moscow subway station; and seized a school in Beslan, a town in Russia near Chechnya, where more than 330 people, many of them children, were killed.

The Limits of Islamism's Appeal

Yet while Islamism succeeded in building large movements and challenging the existing regimes, it failed to make any successful revolutions. The lone exception was Afghanistan, where the Taliban group eventually seized power in the confusion following the Soviet withdrawal. There were many reasons for this failure.

One reason is that Islamist Iran was no utopia. If, as Khomeini claimed, all governments during 1,400 years of Islam had failed, why should his experiment be different? Human nature did not change so easily. Khomeini's Iran, too, was rife with self-seeking leaders, bitter factionalism, and differences of opinion. Groups within the leadership constantly broke up into quarreling factions. While some Iranians benefited from the revolution, many others fled the country. The new regime squandered resources and failed to produce jobs or development, though in this respect it was saved by a massive income from oil. All things considered, Iran's performance was not so great as to encourage emulation.

Even Islamist Iran preferred to sell oil to the industrialized West for hard currency, which it then used to buy the West's superior products. Many of the revolution's leaders had Swiss bank accounts, and their taste for modern comforts was the butt of many jokes in Tehran. When a poor woman complained about the lack of soap powder, ran one popular anecdote, a pro-Khomeini cleric scolded her by saying, "The Prophet Muhammad's daughter didn't have that."

"Yes," replied the woman, "but Muhammad didn't ride around in a Mercedes limousine either."

Iran remained under Islamist rule, but by the 1990s the majority of the population had turned against a government that remained in power by the same measures used by its hated Arab nationalist rivals. In the end, the experience of living under an Islamist regime was the most effective factor in convincing people to oppose Islamism.

But there were many other factors in the failure of Islamism to achieve revolutionary victory. While a common Muslim identity was supposedly going to trump any other loyalty, conflicts among Persians and Arabs, Sunni and Shia Muslims, Iranians and Iraqis, and even adherents of different Islamist groups prevailed over the commonality of Islam. Egyptian or Lebanese Christians, non-Muslim Alawites and Druze, as well as Muslim Kurds and Berbers, saw Islamism as a threat. Iran might claim to be a paragon of Islam, but this did not impress Arabs who saw it as Persian, or Sunni Muslims who saw it as Shia.

Still another set of factors concerned the cleverness of the regimes in fighting off the Islamist challenge. They used a wide variety of stratagems, ranging from repression to co-optation to using their own very significant Islamic assets. Pro-regime clerics criticized Islamism while government officials portrayed themselves as the defenders of Islam—as well as Arab nationalism—against the nefarious forces of imperialism, Zionism, and liberal Arab reformers.

Radical Islamists assassinated Egyptian president Anwar al-Sadat in 1981 and waged a decade-long revolt, but they were soundly defeated. Revolts were also crushed with great loss of life in Algeria and Syria. In Jordan, Islamists were allowed to participate in electoral politics but were kept from achieving more than a limited quota of elected offices. In Lebanon, meanwhile, the Islamist group Hezbollah (the Party of God) became a powerful force, but it could not even gain a monopoly within its own Shia community, much less overcome the opposition of Christians, Druze, and Sunni Muslims. Islamist groups were divided and often fought among themselves.

But perhaps the most significant single factor in the failure of Islamism to spur revolutions was the fact that most Muslims did not accept Islamism as

This photograph was taken on October 6, 1981, moments after radical Islamists opened fire on the reviewing stand at a military parade in Cairo. Their target, Egyptian president Anwar al-Sadat, was killed in the attack. Sadat had angered the Islamists by signing a peace treaty with Israel.

the legitimate, or at least preferable, interpretation of their religion. In theory, of course, all Muslims accepted Islam as the proper organizing principle for their lives and societies. Practice was altogether different. The great majority of traditionalist Muslims rejected Islamism's interpretation of their religion, while less fervent Muslims were horrified by the idea of living in an extremist Muslim society. They might be culturally conservative and pious, yet to them Islamism appeared to be a deviation from the Islam they had always known and practiced.

Among fellow Muslims, the Islamists remained largely on the defensive against the alluring onslaught of modernization and Westernization, with its movies, consumerism, love songs, fashions, delightful merchandise and luxuries, science, and education. Many of their compatriots were not so eager to boycott Western culture or ideas, and an urgent desire for the West's respect infected even the most militant, anti-Western leaders. "The grandeur of the Islamic revolution" was proven, Iran's speaker of parliament Ali Akbar Hashemi Rafsanjani noted proudly, because it impressed the West so much that Iran was now being compared to the Soviet Union and France rather than to mere Third World states like Algeria or Vietnam. Yet this showed precisely the implicit view of many Muslims, even Islamists, that the West was superior in some way.

Iran remained Islamist, but despite its strenuous efforts to obtain nuclear weapons, it did not seem likely to realize its ambitions to spread the revolution abroad. Usually, Iranian policy was also more cautious than Iranian ideology, as officials were concerned that foreign adventurism might endanger their regime's survival at home. At any rate, the Arab and

Muslim world had found new heroes after Khomeini's death in June 1989. These included the Arab nationalist Saddam Hussein and the Saudi terrorist Osama bin Laden. The Iranian Revolution's influence had been powerful enough to spread Islamism, but it had been limited enough not to bring more victories.

(Opposite) Egyptian police search for Muslim extremists in a Cairo slum, 1992. Throughout the 1990s, Islamists sought to overthrow the Egyptian regime, but the government ruthlessly suppressed the insurgency. (Right) Hassan Nasrallah, leader of the Iranian-funded Islamist group Hezbollah, which was formed in 1982 after the Israeli invasion of southern Lebanon.

3 The Spread of Political Islamism

uilding on the philosophy of earlier Islamists, the experience of the war in Afghanistan, and the success of Iran's revolution, a large number of radical Islamist movements developed wherever Muslims lived. In addition to the Middle East, there were significant movements in Asia, Africa, and Europe. By the mid-1980s the most noteworthy opposition groups throughout the Arab world were Islamists. And wherever large Muslim communities came up against other groups—in Indonesia and the Philippines, Thailand and China, Chechnya and Nigeria, even France and Britain—Islamist groups became involved in conflict against the governments and other communities.

In several countries—notably Algeria, Egypt, Iraq, and Syria—Islamist organizations launched ill-fated efforts to seize power. Often, though by no means always, these groups became most widely visible through terrorist attacks. But they also engaged in a huge amount of grassroots organizing and propagandizing. After the turn of the century, more groups also became involved in electoral activity.

Islamist groups ranged from well-organized parties functioning on a national level to underground cells to small circles around individual preachers. Despite its supra-national pretensions, Islamism remained largely tied to national frameworks. The flavor and variety of the emerging movement can best be seen through a variety of case studies.

Algeria

The North African country provides a classic case of a victorious Arab nationalist revolution gone wrong. The National Liberation Front (FLN) forced out the French and achieved independence for Algeria. But thereafter it became a relatively corrupt and ineffective regime, despite the opportunities offered by the country's natural gas reserves. As disillusion set in and after bloody rioting in 1988, the regime decided to hold multiparty elections. The following year, clerics attracted to the philosophy of the Muslim Brotherhood created the Islamic Salvation Front (FIS). The FIS had Islamist goals but used relatively moderate means, building a mass organization and winning 55 percent of the vote in the 1990 local elections. Realizing the danger, the government tried to clamp down on the FIS, which called a general strike in response.

In December 1991, when national elections were held, the FIS won big in the first round of balloting. It was clear that the FIS would gain an absolute majority in the second round. In response the government, urged to be tough by the military, dissolved parliament, cancelled the elections, and banned the FIS. A civil war broke out. By the time it mostly ended eight years later, the conflict had claimed more than 100,000 victims. And during the fighting an even more extreme group emerged from the FIS: the Armed Islamic Group (GIA). The GIA killed peasants who were suspected of being neutral, but both sides fought brutally. In the end, it was clear that, despite the country's massive losses, the Islamists could not win.

The Algerian experience brought three important lessons. First, Arab nationalist regimes were loath to permit Islamists to take over, even through fair elections. Second, a strong Islamist movement could tear a country apart. And third, a determined government and armed forces could defeat an Islamist insurgency no matter how ruthless the revolutionaries might be.

Egypt

Cowed by Nasser's repression and their years in harsh prison camps, members of the Muslim Brotherhood were too cautious to challenge the regime. In the 1970s, however, President Anwar al-Sadat let the group revive to help him in defeating his rivals in the Nasserist left. While still technically illegal, the Brotherhood began to reorganize as a mass organization, campaign for making Islamic law the basis of Egypt's justice system, take over professional associations, and run candidates in elections on the lists of other parties. But smaller groups, impatient and demanding revolution now, constantly evolved out of the Brotherhood's membership. Some—including those who would assassinate Sadat in 1981—tried to launch insurgencies through terrorism. Others focused on mass organizing among students and in neighborhoods.

By 1990, while the Brotherhood still stood aloof, this new generation of Islamists launched an armed struggle against the regime. Officials were assassinated, Egyptian Christians attacked, and foreign tourists murdered. A wave of violence during the decade claimed the lives of several thousand people. Yet Egypt's rulers, like their counterparts in Algeria, were willing to do whatever was necessary to stay in power. The Islamists also made mistakes. Killing fellow Muslims proved unpopular among most Egyptians, while the regime used more moderate clerics to discredit the Islamists' claim to have the proper interpretation of Islam.

By the end of the decade, the insurgency had been defeated. This failure inspired a debate among Egyptian Islamists. Some made a truce with the government and returned to local organizing; others followed bin Laden in shifting their attacks abroad. The Muslim Brotherhood simply tried to avoid repression. Still, periodic harassment of Brotherhood institutions and arrests of its leaders served as reminders of the repression the group would suffer if it exceeded the bounds set by the government.

With the opening of the electoral process in 2005, the Brotherhood took advantage of the opportunity and elected—albeit not under its own banner—20 percent of the members of parliament. To some extent, this situation is to the regime's advantage because many Egyptians, frightened about an Islamist takeover, support the government as the lesser evil. Moreover, the strength of the Islamists shows foreign observers that if they try to foist democracy on a reluctant dictatorship, they might end up with a government more antagonistic to their interests and more destabilizing for the region.

The Egyptian case showed the wide variety of Islamist doctrines and strategies that could coexist. In the face of brutal measures by the regime, Islamists did not even come close to victory. But despite their failure, the Islamists did not give up either.

Iraq

Unlike Algeria and Egypt (but like Lebanon, Syria, and some other places), Iraq saw Islamism within its borders strengthened by having a distinctive communal aspect. The majority of Iraqis were Shia Muslims, but the country was ruled by Sunnis. Islamists and Shias alike were ruthlessly suppressed by the regime of Saddam Hussein, notably during their 1991 rebellion after Saddam's defeat in the Gulf War. Since the 1980s, Shia Islamists had congregated in neighboring Iran, which they supported during the Iran-Iraq War. In 2003, when the United States overthrew Saddam and swept away his Arab nationalist regime, Shia Islamists had a new chance. Since Shias were a majority, a ticket led by Shia clerics and Islamist militias was able to win the elections and write a constitution favoring their community.

But the new Shia leadership was a complex coalition. The top Iraqi Shia Muslim clerics were more Islamic than Islamist. They did not seek an Islamist regime, but simply one that could guarantee the continuing power of their religion and its ability to influence society. Thus, Ayatollah Ali al-Sistani wanted a strong Islamic factor in education and law, yet he was willing to compromise and accept a pluralist, democratic state. At the same time, though, Islamist elements in his coalition did want a total transformation of Iraqi society. Which side would win this competition, or even how open the struggle would be, remained unclear.

Mirroring the communal composition of Iraqi society, there was also a Sunni Islamist sphere in which insurgents—many of them bin Laden supporters—attacked Shia mosques and murdered huge numbers of Shia Muslims, including clerics. The leader of al-Qaeda in Iraq, Abu Musab al-Zarqawi, even went so far as to declare a jihad against Shia Muslims, branding them traitors and heretics. Many of the Islamists fighting in Iraq were not even Iraqi; Zarqawi, for example, was a Jordanian. They viewed the country merely as a front in the international Islamist struggle. But Iraq had become the scene not only of an attempted Islamist revolution but also of a civil war fought mainly between the Sunni and Shia communities.

The 2003 U.S. invasion of Iraq attracted radical Islamists to the country. Among the most notorious was Abu Musab al-Zarqawi (shown here), a Jordanian thug-turned-terrorist whose attacks on Shia Muslims helped ignite a civil war in post-Saddam Iraq.

Jordan

Unlike their counterparts in Algeria, Egypt, and to a lesser extent Iraq, Islamist groups in

Jordan have rarely used violence. Exceptions include small organizations that lack a broad base inside the country (notably al-Qaeda). The main Islamist group within Jordan is the Islamic Action Front, whose history parallels that of the Egyptian Muslim Brotherhood. Unlike the Brotherhood, however, the Jordanian group has a history of close cooperation with the government; it aided King Hussein in his efforts to curb radical Arab nationalists.

The Islamic Action Front is allowed to operate freely in Jordan as long as it does not challenge the monarchy and accepts a quota of parliamentary seats in manipulated elections. In fair balloting the group would receive far more seats. The Islamic Action Front is careful never to call for the regime's overthrow. Much of its energy is devoted to a campaign to get the government to cancel its peace treaty with Israel. A key factor here is the ethnic-communal situation in Jordan. Most of the power is held by "East Bank" Jordanians (members of traditionally nomadic Bedouin tribes or Jordan Valley peasants), yet a majority of the country's citizens are Palestinians. Pessimistic about a victory by the Palestine Liberation Organization (PLO) that would wipe out Israel, many Palestinian Jordanians have turned to the Islamic Action Front. As long as it accepts the system's constraints, however, the Islamic Action Front will never pose a real danger to the Jordanian monarchy or even have a chance of taking power.

In general, the Jordanian situation provides the best example of an Islamist movement that accepts the rules of legality and an electoral process, even though these ensure it will remain in the political minority. Some Jordanian Islamists have joined the international jihad movement (the most notable example was Zarqawi, who was killed in a U.S. air strike in 2006). They launch sporadic terrorist attacks but do not play a major role within Jordan.

Lebanon

In Lebanon, as in Iraq (and Syria), the Islamist movement is totally entwined with ethnic-communal issues. While there have been local Sunni Islamist groups, the most important Islamist organization is the Shia Muslim Hezbollah. Hezbollah, which has been backed by Syria and Iran, seeks to turn Lebanon into a Shia-dominated Islamist state. It also tries to lead the Shia community in the face of communal nationalist rivals. Historically, Hezbollah's appeal has rested on the fact that for decades the Shia were Lebanon's poorest, most neglected, and most underrepresented community. The Shia have also been Lebanon's fastest-growing group, which has inspired Hezbollah to seek power.

Yet given the claims of Christian, Sunni Muslim, and Druze communities, Hezbollah has little chance of taking over the country. It tried to broaden its appeal by wrapping itself in a patriotic mantle as the group most involved in fighting Israel. This worked well as long as Israeli forces were in southern Lebanon (1982–2000). But once the Israelis withdrew, Hezbollah was seen as sustaining a conflict that destabilized Lebanon and damaged its economic reconstruction. In July 2006 Hezbollah militia fighters raided northern Israel, killing three Israeli soldiers and taking two others hostage. This provoked a month-long war with Israel that caused immense destruction in Lebanon, as well as the loss of up to 1,000 lives.

During the summer of 2006, fighting erupted in Lebanon after Hezbollah militants crossed into Israel and seized two Israeli soldiers. Seen here is the aftermath of an Israeli air force bombing raid on Beirut.

Another factor isolating Hezbollah was its opposition to Syria's pressured withdrawal from Lebanon in 2005. The Syrian pullout was greeted enthusiastically by most Lebanese.

Thus, Hezbollah has certain strong assets: its leadership of Lebanon's largest single community, a strong and well-armed militia, and backing from Syria and Iran. But it also has distinct liabilities, especially the uniting of other groups against it and the virtual impossibility of expanding further its existing base of support. In the 2005 elections, Hezbollah did well in its own community and even entered the government, but in political terms it was frequently outmaneuvered. Hezbollah is therefore the best example of an Islamist group as a sectarian-communal leader that uses both terrorism and electoral methods.

Palestinians

As in Lebanon, the major Palestinian Islamist groups—Hamas and Islamic Jihad—try to make the Islamist revolution popular by associating it with a "national liberation" movement against foreign, non-Muslim enemies. In its 1988 charter, Hamas—an outgrowth of local Muslim Brotherhood elements— lays down its basic ideology. Israel is to be wiped off the map and is portrayed as a demonic enemy of God, this hatred merging into a generalized anti-Semitism. Palestinian nationalism, the ideology of the rival PLO, is treated as both a brother and as a less worthy rival. For Hamas, the struggle against non-Muslims is to be a stepping-stone toward mobilizing Muslims, winning their support, taking over leadership of the movement, and eventually becoming the leadership of an Islamist state. Terrorism was the main element in the military strategy of Hamas, which formed in 1987 in support of the first *intifada*, or Palestinian uprising against Israeli occupation in the West Bank and Gaza Strip.

Knowing it was weaker than the nationalists and that it would receive blame for any Palestinian civil war, Hamas dealt cautiously with the PLO. It openly rejected the peace process with Israel during the 1990s and continued to stage terrorist attacks except when strongly pressured by the PLO leadership. Hamas also enjoyed growing support from Iran and Syria, as well as financing by rich Saudis.

But time brought new opportunities. When the PLO organized a second intifada after rejecting peace with Israel in 2000, it cooperated closely with Hamas. And when a weak PLO leadership succeeded the late Yasir Arafat in

These women in Gaza are marching in support of Hamas, a Palestinian organization dedicated to the destruction of Israel.

2004 and held fair elections in 2005, Hamas expanded its base of support. The PLO, having rejected a compromise peace, was unable to bring political benefits to its people. Its corruption and administrative incompetence disenchanted many Palestinians, and a split in Fatah, the main nationalist group, opened the door for a Hamas triumph in the 2006 elections.

Hamas, then, is a case study of an Islamist revolutionary movement that put the emphasis on a "national liberation" approach, both in cooperation and competition with nationalists. It was far from gaining control over the Palestinians—much less destroying Israel. But it had achieved a popular base that was probably proportionally higher than that of any Islamist group in an Arab country.

Saudi Arabia

This country provides the strange spectacle of an Islamist movement trying to overthrow a regime that is both the most Islamic in the world (at least outside of Iran) and the biggest funder of Islamic missionary efforts. In addition, the dominant Wahhabi form of Islam in Saudi Arabia has often been an influence on radical Islamists.

Nevertheless, Osama bin Laden initially became a revolutionary to bring down the Saudi regime. He turned to international terrorism only after this failed. In 1991, shortly after the end of the Gulf War, hard-line Islamists presented a petition to Saudi Arabia's King Fahd. It was signed by hundreds of Islamic clerics and others who had been discussing this project for more than a year. Called the "Letter of Demands," the petition was ostensibly a call to reform phrased in democratic-sounding language. But the goal of the signers was to turn the country into an Islamist state. The government ignored the "Letter of Demands," and bin Laden later characterized this refusal as justification for the Islamist revolutionary movement to overthrow the Saudi regime. Following their attacks on the United States of September 11, 2001, al-Qaeda terrorists carried out many attacks within Saudi Arabia.

Two key points must be borne in mind in analyzing Saudi Islamism. First, while Saudi extreme piety and Wahhabism would seem to insulate the kingdom from an Islamist challenge, this atmosphere—including indoctrination in the educational system and the incendiary sermons preached by Saudi clerics—facilitates the recruitment of Islamist revolutionaries. Indeed, Saudi Arabia has exported both Islamist agitators and, in the case of Iraq, terrorists. Because Saudi Arabia purports to be so pious, any contradictions or lapses are all the more noticed and spark opposition.

Islamist terrorism strikes the United States: smoke billows from the Twin Towers in New York City, September 11, 2001. Al-Qaeda, the organization responsible for the attacks, was established by an exiled Saudi, Osama bin Laden.

Second, only a small minority of radical Islamists in the kingdom actively support bin Laden or the terrorist campaign. Most think the armed struggle is misguided and doomed to fail. Why attack the regime, they argue, when pressure and persuasion can serve the same goal? These Islamists can find members of the royal family as well as leading clerics to support that position. Thus, they seek not to overthrow the regime but to put into positions of power people who would implement the kind of Islamic transformation they believe Saudi Arabia needs. (In general they agree that the kingdom needs fewer changes than other, less pious, Muslim societies.) To preserve itself, the current regime constantly caters to the Islamist lobby, especially avoiding measures that might antagonize the hard-liners.

Saudi Arabia is the only country where Islamists can reasonably believe that the current system may be guided in the direction they want rather than having to be destroyed completely. For those like bin Laden who consider the Saudi dynasty as inevitably corrupt and subservient to the West, however, only a thoroughgoing revolution will suffice.

Syria

As in Iraq and Lebanon, the Islamist movement in Syria was closely linked to communal differences. But in Syria it was a vehicle—though not the only one—for a group, Sunni Muslims, that constituted more than 60 percent of the population. The problem was that an Arab nationalist dictatorship, dominated by non-Muslim Alawites, actually controlled the country and did not hesitate to use the most severe means of repression to defeat the Islamists.

The Islamist movement in Syria arose from the Muslim Brotherhood branches there and long tried to avoid a confrontation with the secular-oriented Arab nationalist regime. In 1982, however, a small clash between an

Islamist band and the Syrian military escalated in the city of Hama. Syrian forces leveled large parts of the city and killed somewhere between 10,000 and 30,000 people, imprisoning Islamist activists across the country. The Islamist movement was brutally crushed—ironically, by a government that was allied with Iran, Hamas, and Hezbollah. None of these allies seemed bothered by this contradiction.

Members of Syria's parliament applaud their country's new president, Bashar al-Assad, July 11, 2000. Assad, who succeeded his father, longtime Syrian dictator Hafez al-Assad, has tried to placate Islamist radicals in his country—a dangerous tactic, Middle East analysts suggest.

When longtime Syrian dictator Hafez al-Assad died and was replaced by his son, Bashar, in 2000, conditions eased slightly as the new leader briefly sought to show that he was more open to change. Political prisoners held for decades were released. Challenged by a nascent pro-democracy movement, however, Bashar quickly clamped down. But he saw the Islamists as a preferred alternative to the reformers and began to let them operate more freely.

However, it was really the 2003 U.S. overthrow of Saddam Hussein in neighboring Iraq that deepened Bashar's new strategy in this regard. To ease domestic dissent, Bashar not only supported the Islamist-based insurgency in Iraq but also took the internal Islamists as his allies. This was a very dangerous approach. For while the Syrian Sunni Islamists put the emphasis on attacking U.S. forces and fighting against the Shia-led government in Iraq, they did little to conceal their intention of turning on Bashar one day. If that were to happen, through fair elections or an armed uprising, regime supporters and the Alawite community in general might face a massacre. Potentially, Syria could be the site of the most devastating Islamist revolution and civil war of any Arab country.

Turkey

Turkey presents an apparent paradox. The country has energetically embraced secularism for more than 80 years. Moreover, it lacks significant international problems and has enjoyed relative success in economic and social development. Turkey is even on the road to being admitted to the European Union as a full partner.

Yet at the onset of the 21st century, it was the first country to have a democratic, moderate Islamic government. In part, this outcome was an accident. The Justice and Development Party (AKP) achieved roughly 25 to 30 percent of the vote against left, center-right, and right-wing nationalist rivals in the 2002 elections. Only Turkey's peculiar electoral system, along with the incredible rivalries and incompetence of its opponents, allowed the AKP to achieve power.

But there were also clear reasons for the AKP's success. Turkey was facing its worst economic recession in modern history, brought on by its leftist nationalist government. The voters knew that the other parties—which had all been tried and found wanting in government—were rife with corruption, arrogance, and incompetence. In contrast, the AKP's founder and leader, Recep Tayyip Erdogan, had done a good job as mayor of Istanbul. The party also found a strong constituency that combined conservative central Anatolians, a rising pious middle class in provincial towns, and village immigrants to big cities who had been battered by cultural dissonance. All these groups felt neglected by the urban secular establishment.

Finally, Erdogan persuaded most Turks that he and the party were not radical Islamists who would challenge the country's relatively secularist lifestyle and constitutional system. There had long been an Islamist party in Turkey, which had even taken power briefly in the previous decade, but it had usually received a small proportion of votes. When it did take power, this Islamist party proved an embarrassing failure and was soon deposed by the military. While the Islamists openly rejected Europe and called for Turkey to turn toward the Muslim states to the east, Erdogan emerged as the

Supporters of Turkey's Justice and Development Party (AKP) celebrate victory in the November 2002 elections. Though its roots were unquestionably Islamist, the AKP tempered its rhetoric—a necessity in Turkey, whose armed forces have a history of removing governments they believe violate the country's tradition of secular politics.

champion of a European orientation. Voters would back a culturally conservative party but not an Islamist one.

The AKP's success was due not only to the fact that it was a Turkish-style movement. It also won because it had made a transition from Islamist to Islamic conservative politics. Even so, there are some in the party who would like to go further. It is doubtful that the Turkish system would permit this to happen. For many reasons, then, Turkey is more a unique case than a model for Islamism elsewhere.

(Opposite) In May 2003 a suicide car bomber killed eight Americans at a housing complex for expatriates in Riyadh, Saudi Arabia. Though Islamists seek to establish conservative Muslim rule in their own countries, their targets are often foreigners. (Right) Fatah al-Islam militants at a Palestinian refugee camp in northern Lebanon. In May 2007 fighting erupted between the Lebanese army and Fatah al-Islam.

4 *Strategies*

slamist movements have employed a variety of tactics, strategies, and forms of organization. What they share is the goal of seizing state power and revolutionizing their societies. They thus have more in common with Western movements like communism and fascism than with such counterparts as liberalism or conservatism.

In this context, there is also an important difference between Islamic forces and Islamist ones. The former are typically conservative and traditionalist and want to preserve their societies as they have been in the recent past. The latter categorically reject that goal in favor of sweeping the old systems away. Yet Islamic and Islamist approaches can be allied, and Islamic activists can be converted to Islamist ones. There are some parallels in their approaches. Islamic forces can try to influence society to be more pious, to maintain conservative ways and resist Western cultural influences. But by definition Islamist forces seek to seize power, as their goal is not a more Muslim society—a return to or preservation of tradition—but the creation of a thoroughly Muslim society, a utopian leap, a rejection of the past. The difference between Islamic and Islamist is thus parallel to the distinction between liberal and Communist or conservative and Fascist.

It is certainly possible that Islamic democratic parties—similar to the Christian Democratic parties of Italy and other European countries—may one day develop. But these would emerge either from conservative, traditionalist-oriented Islamic forces or from Islamists who rejected that creed.

Contemporary Debates

A number of important debates and distinctions have sprung up in Islamist movements. Radical Islamism does not require the use of terrorism as a central tactic. Various Islamist movements have not used political violence of this nature. There is, however, some inclination toward that approach, since Islamists regard themselves as having a monopoly of truth and demonize their opponents as enemies of God. Even Islamist movements that have not employed terrorism directly use the most violent rhetoric and threats while applauding others who employ terrorism.

Some groups justify the use of terrorism against fellow Muslims. These groups include al-Qaeda, the Algerian GIA, and the Egyptian revolutionary groups of the 1980s and 1990s. Others reject this idea, however, and focus on rationalizing terrorism against non-Muslims: Westerners, Israelis, Jews, Christians, and Hindus.

A second set of issues revolves around what might be called jihadism versus revolution. Many Islamists—and this was certainly the priority of the 1980s and 1990s—put the emphasis on overthrowing the regime ruling their

A 2007 rally in Tehran marking the anniversary of the Islamic Revolution. Nearly three decades after the overthrow of the U.S.-backed shah, the United States remains a target of the Iranian government's vitriol—though analysts suggest that many Iranians, particularly the young, have a much more positive view of America.

country. The failure of these revolutionary efforts, however, sparked a shift among some Islamists. They increasingly advocated making attacks against foreign targets a priority. Favorite targets of these jihadists included the West and Israel.

This shift was rationalized by a set of arguments grounded in the Islamist worldview. A central point is that the power of the West makes it impossible to overthrow governments like those in Saudi Arabia and Egypt. Thus, the argument goes, it is necessary to first intimidate, defeat, and drive out Western influence and destroy Israel (the far enemy) in order to revolutionize Muslim societies by overthrowing their corrupt regimes (the near enemy).

Moreover, it is claimed that the West and Israel—in a Christian-Jewish and imperialist-Zionist conspiracy—are attacking and trying to destroy the Muslims. Therefore, jihad—including the targeting of civilians—is merely a matter of self-defense and is thus justified under classical Islamic practice.

The jihadist approach is also attractive for other reasons. Attacking and killing fellow Muslims while claiming that Islam as currently practiced is heretical will not help Islamists win the hearts and minds of fellow Muslims. Killing non-Muslims is simply more popular and less controversial. Hezbollah and Hamas (which could portray themselves as "national liberation" movements) ranked among the most successful Islamist groups because they carried on terrorism against Israel. A large proportion of Muslims—arguably a majority—will support such activities, at least tacitly.

Exporting the struggle also reduces the incentive of Arab and other regimes to repress radical Islamists. Such regimes, in fact, may cheer on the efforts of radical Islamists and even provide them with assistance. Thus, the war in Iraq—nominally against Western occupiers but often against Shia Muslims—became very popular among many Muslims. In various ways, Iran, Syria, and Saudi Arabia, as well as almost all the Arab media, facilitated and endorsed the Islamist terrorist campaign there.

At the same time, though, some Islamists who put a priority on internal revolution criticized the jihadist approach. They claimed that this shift was a sellout that let impious regimes off the hook. They also noted that once terrorism shifted against the West, Islamists lost former safe havens in Europe and elsewhere as arrests were made and leaders deported out of fear that they would foment terrorism in their host countries. The U.S.-led "war on terrorism" also cut into financial networks and operational capability.

A third set of issues concerns the relationship between Islamist groups and foreign governments. The possibility that Islamist groups may be used by one state against another adds an important dimension to Middle East politics. Three such groups—Hamas and Islamic Jihad among Palestinians, and Hezbollah—receive backing from Iran and Syria, as well as significant funding from Saudis. A number of Islamist groups in the Arab countries bordering the Persian Gulf, and especially Iraq, have also received help from Iran. The insurgents in Iraq obtain assistance also from Syria. In the past, Libya has supplied money and help to Islamist groups in such diverse places as Sudan, the southern Philippines, and sub-Saharan Africa.

To what extent al-Qaeda had contacts with Arab governments is highly controversial. But it does seem clear that Iran and Syria facilitated the escape of leading al-Qaeda terrorists from Afghanistan and aided their safe passage to Lebanon and other countries. At times in the past, militants of the Syrian Muslim Brotherhood have been helped by Jordan; Syria may return the favor by its own covert efforts. An especially important example is Pakistan's use of radical Islamist groups against India, particularly those groups involved in trying to take over Kashmir and join it to Pakistan.

Islamic and Islamist groups tend to be strongest when religious and ethno-national identity joins together. Aside from examples like the ones ana-

Indian troops carry the body of an Islamic militant in Srinagar, the summer capital of Jammu and Kashmir. Pakistan, which lays claim to the Kashmir region, has supported Islamist terrorists who oppose Indian rule.

lyzed above—as in Iraq, Syria, and among Palestinians—there are other such cases outside the Middle East. For example, Islam is the religion of the Uighur people in northwest China, of the Moros in the southern Philippines, and of Malays in Malaysia. As such it is a potent political weapon combining national and religious identity.

Islamist groups have also become involved in a wide range of international conflicts. Even a short list includes the struggle for power in Indonesia; regional insurgencies against the Philippines, Russia, Thailand, China, and India; organizing and terrorism in a wide variety of European states; and communal conflicts in Nigeria, Sudan, and, to a lesser extent, Bosnia and Kosovo. Indeed, it is probably accurate to say that Islamist radical groups are at present the main global source not only of terrorism but also of instability and political violence generally. Significant Islamist political activity has taken place in more than 30 percent of the world's countries. Political Islam has been active in Australia, Asia, Europe, the Middle East, African countries such as Nigeria and Kenya, and North America.

The Many Activities of Islamist Groups

Yet Islamist groups in all these places do far more than engage in terrorism. Their activities are as varied as those of virtually any other political organization. Among them are:

Charitable efforts. To build a base of support and service their constituencies, Islamist groups provide relief to the poor, money to support the families of those killed in warfare, and other aid. In Egypt, for example, Islamist groups have provided low-cost used textbooks to university students. In performing these kinds of activities, the groups not only give benefits to their supporters—and thus strengthen the loyalty of existing supporters while recruiting new ones—but also step in where government fails to provide for social welfare. This sends the message that the Islamist groups are morally superior to the regimes. It also creates, albeit on a small scale, an incipient Islamist state, which is intended to show how people would be better off living in that type of society. Funds raised for nominally charitable activities, however, are often diverted to finance terrorist operations.

Mosque efforts. When Islamist movements control specific mosques and have the backing of respected and popular preachers, they enjoy a key asset. Even in authoritarian states, the mosque and religious instruction are areas—often the sole ones—that the rulers cannot completely control. Indeed, in many countries most mosques and religious schools come at least nominally under government ministries—for instance, in the key areas of hiring and firing teachers or clerics. Preachers have frequently given sermons reflecting Islamist ideas or even endorsing specific groups, while religious teachers have indoctrinated students.

Campaign posters and banners adorn the exterior of a mosque in Ramallah, in the Palestinian-administered West Bank. Even in authoritarian states, rulers cannot completely control the political messages that come from mosques.

Even in non-Islamist countries, the educational and religious sectors have often been influenced or controlled by Islamist or pro-Islamist government officials. In Kuwait, one such individual later emerged as bin Laden's spokesman. In Saudi Arabia, a mother recounted how her sons were told to celebrate the September 11 attacks by a teacher who later became a leader in the armed insurgency against the government.

Attempts to take over professional associations. In countries like Egypt and Jordan, associations of lawyers, doctors, teachers, engineers, students, and others are led by Islamists. These influential people can be mobilized as activists in the movement and are in a good position to spread its message. The idea that Islamists recruit mainly among the poor and unemployed is mistaken.

Media activities. While many governments in the Muslim world control radio, television, newspapers, and book publishing, Islamist groups have tried to create their own assets in the media wherever possible. There is substantial Islamist influence on satellite television networks, including Al Jazeera television.

Fund-raising efforts. Aside from charitable activities, both in Muslim-majority countries and in the West, Islamist groups raise money directly to support armed struggles. This is especially the case when the war is being waged against non-Muslims—as against Israel and American forces in

Iraq—and thus is more likely to enjoy governmental tolerance and public support. In Saudi Arabia, for example, telethons and public appeals have been organized to finance Hamas. Funds may also be raised as protection money, since those giving may fear they will themselves be attacked if they do not provide such support. In some cases, business enterprises may be set up as fronts or to finance Islamist groups. This is especially true of the Islamic banking sector, which promises to handle investors' money in a

Newsroom at the Al Jazeera television network, Doha, Qatar. Critics charge that the Arabic-language network, launched in 1996, provides a platform for Islamist extremists.

proper Islamic manner. In a number of cases, however— for example, in Egypt—such banks have turned out to be scams defrauding investors.

Youth activities. In addition to general work in education, Islamist groups often organize youth centers and activities, including religious education and physical education courses. These serve as vehicles for recruiting youth; talent spotters can pick out good candidates for suicide bombing or for joining underground military wings. Where possible, paramilitary training is also conducted and militias formed.

Electoral politics. Islamists hold conflicting attitudes toward elections. Some, like Zarqawi, have opposed participation in elections in principle, arguing that obedience to the demands of God should not be decided by a majority of people and their elected representatives. Others, like the influential Brotherhood ideologue Yusuf al-Qaradawi, an Egyptian who lives in Qatar, favor involvement in electoral politics. Qaradawi has claimed that since Islamists are likely to win elections—they certainly have more followers than liberal reformers—they would be foolish not to take advantage of the opportunity.

There are two kinds of elections in which Islamists might participate. On one hand, there are fixed elections, such as those in Egypt and Jordan. In these contests the regimes give Islamists a share of seats but ensure that they cannot win outright. Despite this fact, the largest Islamist groups have eagerly run candidates to the extent they have been allowed. This reflects both strategic flexibility (to seize any chance, however limited, to promote their cause) and perhaps opportunism (to obtain offices and benefits for leaders).

On the other hand, there are fair elections, like those held in Turkey, Lebanon, Kuwait, Iraq, and Algeria, as well as for the Palestinian Authority. In these elections Islamists have a real chance of winning a share of power, or even of gaining control of the government. Here, too, Islamist groups have participated.

Al-Qaeda and a number of small local groups reject elections in principle. It must be noted, however, that this stance is often intensified by the fact that they could not win.

The willingness of other Islamist groups to participate in elections also depends on their prospects for winning. Sometimes there is a communal aspect to this situation. During the post-Saddam elections in Iraq, for example, Shia Islamists favored participation because they knew that the size of the Shia community (60 to 65 percent of the population) would virtually ensure victory. By contrast, Iraqi Sunni Islamists opposed participation in the elections, as the Sunni Arab share of the population (only about 20 percent) offered them little chance of winning at the polls.

Moderate Islamism?

An important question arises regarding Islamists who gain power, through elections or by other means: Is their approach likely to moderate once they are in control? Many Western observers reason that such an outcome is inevitable. Yet the actual history of Islamist regimes that have attained power in Iran and Afghanistan—as well as experience with such other ideological radicals as Communists and Fascists—shows that this is not at all the case. The Islamists believe that they can substitute repression, mobilization, and ideological fervor for high living standards and other material benefits for citizens. Moreover, they understand that their very militancy and readiness to use violence is their strongest card. Because they believe God has commanded them to take power and use it to realize divine plans on earth, they are unlikely to yield power to those they deem enemies of God and allies of the Devil.

It is possible that Islamic conservative forces could come to accept democratic norms, but Islamists will do so only if they cease to be Islamists. Such an eventuality would require three criteria: they would need to break decisively and clearly with their past; they would need a strong leadership with a clear alternative moderate program; and they would have to expel those who remain radical Islamists. In short, for a moderate Islamic party to develop, it must be clearly a moderate party. Such a change must happen before—rather than after—victory. Otherwise supporters will believe that the victory was gained on the basis of a radical agenda. The same applies to the use of terrorism.

Most of all, they must give up the idea of transforming society totally and permanently. This is what has happened with those leading the Turkish and Iraqi governments—although those governments still have some Islamists in their ranks, who might harbor plans for a future revolution.

A useful evaluation of Islamism, therefore, cannot be based on wishful thinking or an evaluation of the real or synthetic grievances Islamists present. There are many alternatives to dealing with the problems of their countries and communities, and the first of these is to institute democracy and pragmatic developmental efforts. Nationalism and conservative-traditionalist Islam are also viable options. Islamists are involved in a protracted struggle. Although they are unlikely to win, their efforts could engulf large parts of the world in violence and tragedy for many decades to come. This may prove to be the principal political drama and crisis of our era.

1929: Hasan al-Banna creates the Muslim Brotherhood in Egypt; branches in other countries are later formed.

1949: Hasan al-Banna is gunned down in the streets of Cairo on February 12.

1954: After a Muslim Brotherhood member unsuccessfully attempts to assassinate Egypt's president, Gamal Abdel Nasser, the group is outlawed and ruthlessly suppressed.

1964: A few months after making a speech against the dependence of the shah's regime on foreign powers, Ayatollah Ruhollah Khomeini is deported from Iran.

1966: After he proclaims that Egypt under Nasser is not a true Islamic state and should be overthrown, Sayyid Qutb, the most important theorist of revolutionary Islamism, is executed on August 29.

1978: Disaffection with the regime of Iran's shah gathers momentum after government troops fire on demonstrators in Tehran in September.

1979: In February, Ayatollah Khomeini returns to Tehran from exile in Paris to a joyous and massive welcome. Khomeini consolidates power, and on April 1 the Islamic Republic of Iran is proclaimed. In November, Iranian militants seize the U.S. embassy in Tehran.

1981: On October 6, Sadat is shot to death by al-Jihad terrorists, one of them a lieutenant colonel in Egypt's army.

1982: Following an Israeli invasion of southern Lebanon, Hezbollah forms—with the financial support of Iran—as an umbrella organization of various radical Shia groups. In July, Syria's armed forces destroy the Muslim Brotherhood there, killing and arresting thousands of people.

1987: The Palestinian Islamist group Hamas is founded with the goal of destroying Israel.

1988: Osama bin Laden forms the Islamist group al-Qaeda.

1991: Bin Laden flees Saudi Arabia and establishes a base in Sudan. After an Islamist party, the Islamic Salvation Front (FIS), wins the first round of parliamentary elections in Algeria, the military nullifies the vote and bans the FIS, sparking a protracted and bloody conflict with a more radical organization, the Armed Islamic Group (GIA).

1992: The Communist government in Afghanistan is overthrown as Islamist Afghan guerrilla leaders take control of Kabul and declare the Islamic State of Afghanistan.

1993: Jemaah Islamiyah is founded in Malaysia; it is committed to the creation of an Islamist state across Southeast Asia to include Singapore, Indonesia, Malaysia, Brunei, southern Thailand, and southern Philippines.

1994: In December, Russian troops enter Chechnya to quash an independence movement among Muslim Chechens, sparking a brutal 20-month war that claims the lives of up to 100,000 people.

1996: Osama bin Laden issues a "declaration of war" against Christians and Jews throughout the world. In Afghanistan the Taliban take control of Kabul, the capital, and enforce an especially harsh form of Sharia.

1998: In February, bin Laden announces the creation of the "International Islamic Front for Jihad Against the Jews and Crusaders," which includes a number of radical Islamist groups; it proclaims that killing Americans and their allies is the duty of every Muslim.

1999:   The FIS announces that it is calling a halt to its fight against the Algerian government in return for amnesty for its fighters.

2001:   On September 11, al-Qaeda terrorists fly two hijacked jetliners into New York City's World Trade Center and one into the Pentagon, outside Washington, D.C.; a fourth hijacked plane crashes in a field in western Pennsylvania. In all, some 3,000 people are killed. In October, U.S. forces invade Afghanistan—which offers sanctuary to bin Laden and other al-Qaeda members—quickly toppling the Taliban government.

2002:   The Islamic AKP party wins elections in Turkey and forms a government.

2003:   American forces invade Iraq and quickly topple the regime of Saddam Hussein, but a violent insurgency—including participation from foreign Islamist fighters—soon develops.

2005:   Hezbollah wins most of the Shia Muslim vote in Lebanese elections and enters the government, though it soon suspends its participation.

2006:   In July, Hezbollah militants infiltrate northern Israel, kill three Israeli soldiers, and take two others hostage. This ignites a month-long war that causes massive destruction in Lebanon and claims as many as 1,000 lives.

2007:   In May, fighting erupts between Lebanese army troops and militia fighters of Fatah al-Islam—a radical Sunni group believed to be linked to al-Qaeda—near a Palestinian refugee camp.

Arab nationalism—the ideology, which has prevailed in the Arab world since the 1950s, that puts a primacy on Arab rather than Muslim identity and advocates the uniting of all Arab states into one country.

ijtihad—an Islamic tenet (abandoned in the Middle Ages) in which qualified scholars could interpret Muslim law and tradition through analysis and logic.

Islamism—a political philosophy that seeks to attain state power in order to create a society in which Islam, according to the interpretation of the movement, is supreme in all matters.

jahiliyya—the state of paganism that was traditionally said by Muslims to characterize pre-Islamic societies but that Islamists now say also characterizes contemporary Muslim societies, which they view as insufficiently pious.

jihad—a holy war against non-Muslims, seen by Islamists as one of the main duties of all believing Muslims.

jihadist—one who is engaged in jihad, especially an Islamist who argues that an attack on Western targets should be a higher priority than revolution against the regimes ruling Muslim societies because only the defeat of the former, the "far enemy," can make possible the overthrow of the latter, the "near enemy."

Qur'an—Islam's holy scriptures, a key source of Islamic law and practice.

Shia—the smaller of Islam's two major branches, whose rift with the larger Sunni branch originated with seventh-century disputes over who should succeed the prophet Muhammad as leader of the Muslim community. Shia make up the majority in Iran, Iraq, and Bahrain and are the largest single communal group in Lebanon.

Sunni—a Muslim belonging to the orthodox, majority branch of Islam.

takfir——the labeling of other Muslims as heretics and pagans, often to justify attacks on them.

Wahhabism——an extremely conservative form of Islam, dominant in Saudi Arabia and Qatar, that insists on a literal interpretation of the Qur'an and regards all people with different views, including Muslims, as enemies of Islam.

Clawson, Patrick, and Michael Rubin. *Eternal Iran: Continuity and Chaos.* New York: Palgrave Macmillan, 2005.

Rubin, Barry. *Islamic Fundamentalism in Egyptian Politics.* 2nd rev. ed. New York: Palgrave Macmillan, 2002.

———. *Paved with Good Intentions: The American Experience and Iran.* New York: Oxford University Press, 1980.

———. *The Long War for Freedom: The Arab Struggle for Democracy in the Middle East.* Hoboken, N.J.: John Wiley and Sons, 2005.

———. *The Tragedy of the Middle East.* Cambridge, UK: Cambridge University Press, 2002.

Rubin, Barry, and Judith Colp Rubin, editors. *Anti-American Terrorism and the Middle East.* New York: Oxford University Press, 2002.

http://meria.idc.ac.il/journal/1999/issue1/jv3n1a2.html.

Ali Abootalebi, "Islam and Democracy."

http://meria.idc.ac.il/journal/2004/issue4/jv8no4a4.html

Thomas Butko, "Unity Through Opposition: Islam as an Instrument of Radical Political Change."

http://meria.idc.ac.il/journal/2002/issue3/jv6n3a6.html

Reuven Paz, "Middle East Islamism in the European Arena."

http://meria.idc.ac.il/journal/2003/issue4/jv7n4a5.html

Reuven Paz, "Islamists and Anti-Americanism."

http://meria.idc.ac.il/journal/2001/issue4/jv5n4a2.htm

David Zeidan, "The Islamic Fundamentalist View of Life as a Perennial Battle."

Abu Sayyaf group, 35–36
Afghanistan, 20, 21, 34, 36, 76
Al Jazeera (television network), 72, *73*
al-Qaeda, 48, 49, 55, 64, 67–68, 75
   See also bin Laden, Osama
Algeria, 38, 44–45, 64, 75
anti-Westernism, *17*, 20–21, 25–26, 40, 66
   and the Iranian Revolution (1979), 29–30
Arafat, Yasir, 53–54
Armed Islamic Group (GIA), 45, 64
al-Assad, Bashar, *57*, 58
al-Assad, Hafez, *57*, 58
Azzam, Abdallah, 34

al-Banna, Hasan, 24
bin Laden, Osama, 18, 20, 21, 34, 41, 46, 48, 54–55, 56, 72
   See also al-Qaeda

Carter, Jimmy, *29*
charitable efforts, 69–70
   See also strategies, Islamist
Chechnya, 23, *35*, 36

Egypt, 24, 44, 45–47, 66, 70
Erdogan, Recep Tayyip, 59–61

Fahd (King), 54
Fatah al-Islam, 54, *63*
fund-raising, 72–74
   See also strategies, Islamist

Great Mosque, 9

Hamas, 52–54, 57, 66, 67, 73
Heggy, Tarek, 14, 15
Hezbollah, 38, *43*, 50–52, 57, 66, 67
hostage crisis, *29*, 30–31
   See also Iranian Revolution (1979)
Hussein, 32
Hussein (King), 49
Hussein, Saddam, 31–33, 41, 47, 58

ijtihad, 15
Indonesia, 23
Iran, 20, 50, 53, 57, 67, 76
   and the Iranian Revolution (1979), 21, 25–31, 37, 40–41, *65*
Iran-Iraq War, 31–34, 47
Iranian Revolution (1979), 21, 25–28, 37, 40–41
   and the United States, 28–31, *65*
Iraq, 44, 47–48, 58, 67, 75

Islam
   founding and "golden age," 9–13
   and Sharia (law), 25
   Shia and Sunni, *11*, 12, 20, 31–32, 37–38, 47–48, 50, 56, 58, 75
   Wahhabi, 18, 20, 54–55
   See also Islamism; Islamist groups
Islamic Action Front, 49
Islamic Jihad, 52, 67
Islamic Salvation Front (FIS), 44–45
Islamism, 9, 12, 36–41
   in Afghanistan, 20, 21, 34, 36, 76
   in Algeria, 38, 44–45, 64, 75
   and conservatism, 13–16
   definition of, 16–18, 20–21
   in Egypt, 24, 44, 45–47, 66, 70
   history of, 23–25
   in Iraq, 44, 47–48, 58, 67, 75
   in Jordan, 24, 38, 48–50, 68
   in Lebanon, 38, *43*, 50–52, *63*, 75
   moderate, 75–77
   and the Palestinians, *19*, 49, 52–54, *63*, 67, 75
   and politics, 15–16, 43–44,

Numbers in **bold italic** refer to captions.

Contributors

Barry Rubin is director of the Global Research in International Affairs (GLORIA) Center of the Interdisciplinary University. He is editor of the *Middle East Review of International Affairs (MERIA) Journal*.

Picture Credits